PLATEOSAURUS

AND OTHER EARLY LONG-NECKED PLANT-EATERS

Prehistoric World
PLATEOSAURUS
AND OTHER EARLY LONG-NECKED PLANT-EATERS

VIRGINIA SCHOMP

mc Marshall Cavendish Benchmark

New York

Contents

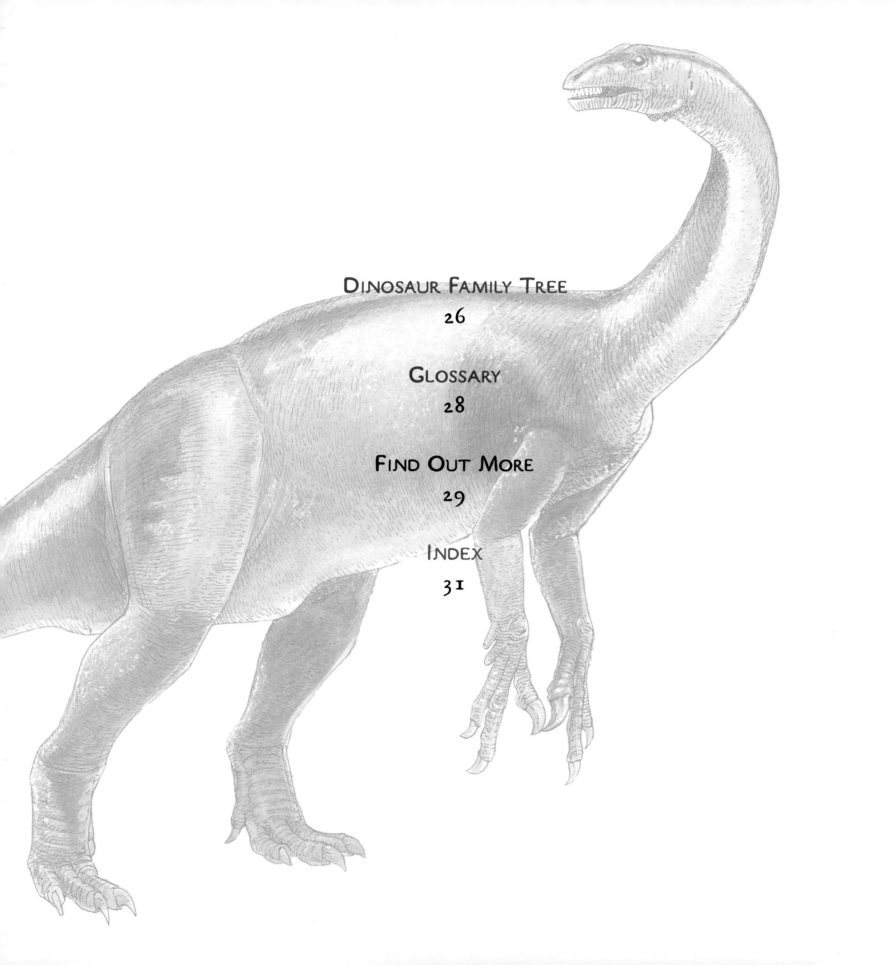

MEET THE LONG-NECKS

The sun beats down on a dusty plain in prehistoric Germany. Small furry creatures nibble on plants beside a muddy water hole. Suddenly the ground shakes. The little animals scatter as a herd of *Plateosaurus* stomps into view. These massive dinosaurs have huge bodies and long, heavy tails. Their long necks sweep over the ground as they search for food. Smashing their way through the vegetation, they gobble up everything in sight. Finally, the dinosaurs move on, leaving nothing but scraps for the smaller plant-eaters.

A herd of hungry Plateosaurus *searches for food beside a prehistoric riverbank.*

You have probably heard of the amazing sauropods. These long-necked plant-eating dinosaurs were the largest land animals that ever lived. But have you met the prosauropods? The name of this group of dinosaurs means "before sauropods." Millions of years before sauropods walked the earth, *Plateosaurus* and its prosauropod cousins were the giants of the animal world.

Brachiosaurus

Apatosaurus

Plateosaurus

You have probably heard of the amazing sauropods. se long-necked plant-eating dinosaurs were the largest animals that ever lived. But have you met the auropods? The name of this group of dinosaurs means ore sauropods." Millions of years before sauropods ked the earth, *Plateosaurus* and its prosauropod ins were the giants of the animal world.

Brachiosaurus

Apatosaurus

saurus

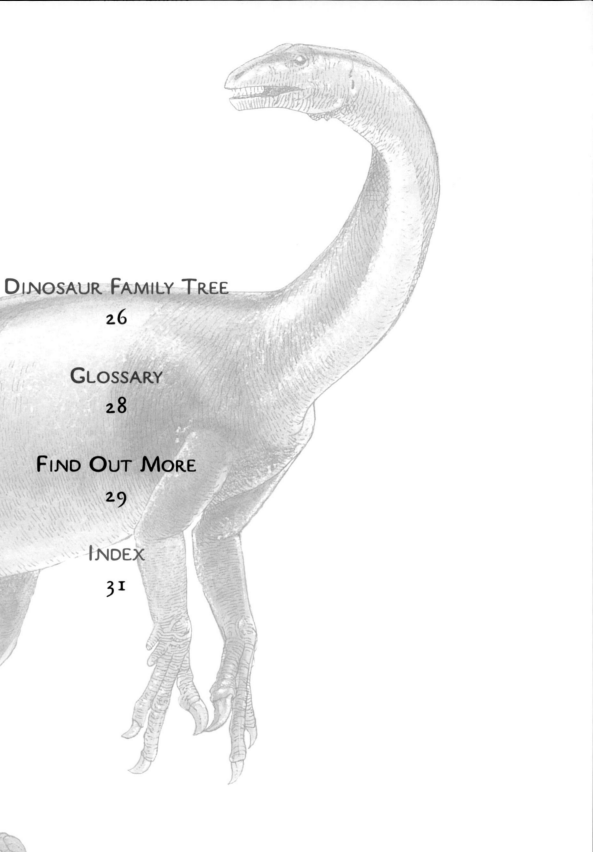

MEET THE LONG-NECKS

The sun beats down on a dusty plain in prehistoric Germany. Small furry creatures nibble on plants beside a muddy water hole. Suddenly the ground shakes. The little animals scatter as a herd of *Plateosaurus* stomps into view. These massive dinosaurs have huge bodies and long, heavy tails. Their long necks sweep over the ground as they search for food. Smashing their way through the vegetation, they gobble up everything in sight. Finally, the dinosaurs move on, leaving nothing but scraps for the smaller plant-eaters.

A herd of hungry Plateosaurus *searches for food beside a prehistoric riverbank.*

The prosauropods never got as big as the sauropods. In other ways, though, the two groups of dinosaurs looked very much alike. In fact, many scientists think that the prosauropods were the great-great-great-grandparents of the sauropods. The chart on page 26 shows how these experts fit the long-necked plant-eaters into the dinosaur family tree. .

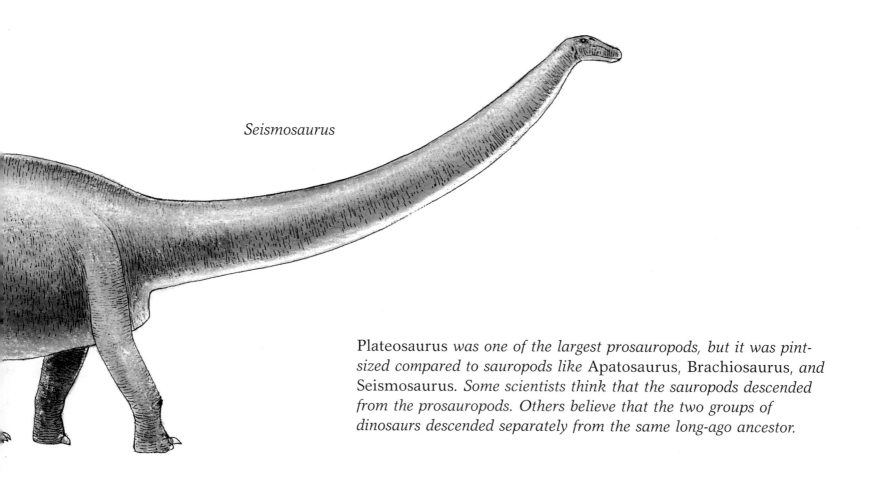

Seismosaurus

Plateosaurus *was one of the largest prosauropods, but it was pint-sized compared to sauropods like* Apatosaurus, Brachiosaurus, *and* Seismosaurus. *Some scientists think that the sauropods descended from the prosauropods. Others believe that the two groups of dinosaurs descended separately from the same long-ago ancestor.*

HEADS ABOVE THE REST

Prosauropods appeared about 230 million years ago, during the long stretch of earth's history known as the Triassic period. They were the first animals tall enough to feed on high tree branches. That gave them a big advantage over smaller plant-eaters. Different types of prosauropod dinosaurs quickly multiplied all over the world.

> **RIOJASAURUS**
> (ree-oh-ha-SORE-us)
> **When:** Late Triassic, 210–205 million years ago
> **Where:** Argentina
> ◆ One of the largest known prosauropods
> ◆ Up to 36 feet long—about as long as a school bus

Massive Riojasaurus *probably spent most of its time on all fours. Like other prosauropods, it also may have stood on its hind legs to feed from high tree branches.*

All prosauropods shared the same basic shape. They had big rounded bodies, small heads, and long necks and tails. The smallest of these dinosaurs were no bigger than a panther. The largest were as heavy as an elephant and as long as a bus.

The Age of Dinosaurs

Dinosaurs walked the earth during the Mesozoic era, also known as the Age of Dinosaurs. The Mesozoic era lasted from about 250 million to 65 million years ago. It is divided into three periods: Triassic, Jurassic, and Cretaceous. (Note: *In the chart, MYA stands for "million years ago."*)

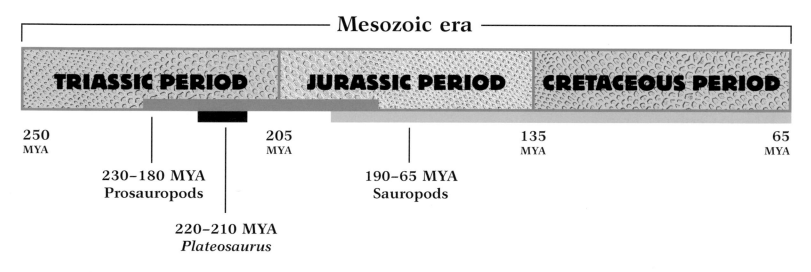

Mesozoic era

TRIASSIC PERIOD   **JURASSIC PERIOD**   **CRETACEOUS PERIOD**

250 MYA   205 MYA   135 MYA   65 MYA

230–180 MYA
Prosauropods

190–65 MYA
Sauropods

220–210 MYA
Plateosaurus

A BIG EATER

Plateosaurus was one of the earliest prosauropods. It was also one of the largest. This four-ton plant-eater was nearly as long as a fire engine. About half of its length was made up of its neck and tail.

Plateosaurus's sturdy back legs were almost twice as long as its front legs. The dinosaur may have stood up on its back legs to reach leafy branches as high as thirteen feet above the ground. When it reared up, it could use its hands to grasp tree trunks and branches. When it walked on all fours, its fingers bent backward to help carry its great weight.

PLATEOSAURUS
(play-tee-oh-SORE-us)
When: Late Triassic, 220–210 million years ago
Where: Germany, France, Switzerland
- Up to 30 feet long—about as long as a pumper truck
- Name means "flat lizard" (for its flat-sided teeth)

Plateosaurus *was one of the first really big dinosaurs. Its strong and flexible hands were designed for many tasks, including walking and gathering food.*

TRIASSIC TIMES

The world of the prosauropods was very different from our world today. During the Triassic period, all the earth's landmasses were joined together in a huge "supercontinent" called Pangaea. Animals could walk from one part of Pangaea to another. The early long-necked plant-eaters made their way to every corner of the world.

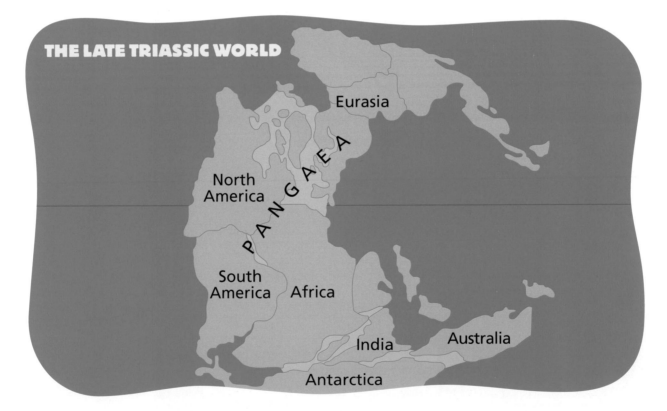

The dark green outlines on the map show the shape of the modern continents. The green shading shows their position during the Late Triassic period, when prosauropods walked the earth.

Stubby ferns and treelike plants cluster around a water hole in a Triassic landscape.

A DESERT HOME

Let's take a tour of *Plateosaurus*'s world. We must travel back 220 million years, to a desertlike region in Europe. The climate is hot and dry. A narrow stream wanders down from the mountains, ending in a shallow lake. Ferns and short treelike plants with tough trunks and leaves grow by the water. These plants have deep roots to help them survive during the long dry seasons of the Triassic period.

A variety of animals share this prehistoric home. We can see frogs, lizards, turtles, and small mouselike mammals. Large mammal-like reptiles chomp on leaves and twigs. Flying reptiles called pterosaurs soar overhead.

Before the dinosaurs, the most common land animals were the mammal-like reptiles. This large and varied group included furry meat-eaters, scaly plant-eaters, and a host of other odd-looking creatures.

Another group of animals has just recently appeared on earth. They are the first dinosaurs. Most of these newcomers are small, swift, two-legged creatures. There are peaceful plant-eaters and sharp-toothed meat-eaters with a taste for lizards and insects. Towering over them all are the long-necked, big-bellied, always-hungry prosauropods.

THECODONTOSAURUS
(THEE-koh-don-tuh-sore-us)
When: Late Triassic,
225–210 million years ago
Where: England and Wales
◆ One of the first dinosaurs discovered and named
◆ Legs about twice as long as arms

Thecodontosaurus *was one of several prosauropods that lived in prehistoric Europe around the same time as* Plateosaurus.

STOMACH STONES

Prosauropods had terrible table manners. Their small, rough-edged, diamond-shaped teeth were good at tearing leaves and twigs from plants, but they weren't made for chewing. The dinosaurs probably gulped down one mouthful of shredded plants after another.

All that vegetation was hard to digest. So prosauropods added an unusual "dessert" to their diet. They swallowed rocks! These "stomach stones" rattled around in the dinosaurs' big bellies and helped mash their meals to a pulp.

This cutaway view of a long-necked plant-eater shows the chambers of its stomach and the gastroliths, or stomach stones, that helped grind up the dinosaur's food.

A HUNGRY HERD

During our prehistoric journey, we might see a small herd of *Plateosaurus.* The plant-eaters are wandering the landscape, searching for food. Prosauropods must eat for many hours each day to nourish their big bulky bodies.

Soon the herd finds a patch of tasty greens. There are ferns, short palmlike cycads, and tall trees called conifers. The dinosaurs slowly sweep their long necks over the ground and up to the treetops. Their small, rough-edged teeth strip the leaves, twigs, and needles from the low-growing plants and tree branches.

The top of one tall conifer is out of reach. Tilting up on its hind legs, a hungry *Plateosaurus* reaches out with its hands. It uses the long, curved claws on its thumbs to hook the high branches and drag them down to its mouth.

With its long neck, Massospondylus *could reach high into the trees. This dinosaur's strong, flexible hands were useful for grasping as well as walking.*

> **MASSOSPONDYLUS**
> (mass-oh-SPON-die-lus)
> **When:** Early Jurassic,
> 205–190 million years ago
> **Where:** Southern Africa and
> North America
> ◆ Longer neck than most prosauropods
> ◆ Very small head with long upper jaw

DINOSAUR DEFENSES

In Triassic times, most meat-eating animals were fairly small. Even the hungriest meat-eater would think twice before attacking a herd of towering *Plateosaurus.* When danger did threaten, the plant-eaters had several defenses. They could run away. They could try to whack the attacker with their heavy tails. Prosauropods may even have used their long sharp thumb claws to jab and stab their enemies.

Baby prosauropods were too small and weak to defend themselves. However, parents probably took good care of their young. When the dinosaurs traveled or rested, the adults stayed on the outside of the herd. The youngsters remained safely in the middle.

This tiny Mussaurus *has just hatched from its egg. Scientists have found many fossils of* Mussaurus *eggs, nests, and babies.*

MUSSAURUS
(muh-SORE-us)
When: Late Triassic, 215 million years ago
Where: Argentina
◆ About the size of a puppy
◆ Name means "mouse lizard"

THE NEW GIANTS

Prosauropods walked the earth for about 50 million years. Then, as the Triassic period gave way to the Jurassic period, they began to die out. Some scientists think that the early long-necked plant-eaters were pushed aside when the sauropod dinosaurs appeared.

Little Anchisaurus *was one of the last surviving prosauropods. This eight-foot-long dinosaur lived alongside some of the first giant long-necked sauropods.*

Sauropods were much bigger than prosauropods. They could reach higher branches and consume much more food. These awesome long-necked giants would survive right up to the end of the Age of Dinosaurs.

ANCHISAURUS
(an-kee-SORE-us)
When: Early Jurassic, 190 million years ago
Where: Connecticut and Massachusetts
♦ First dinosaur discovered in North America
♦ Weighed 60 pounds—about as much as a collie

Dinosaur Family Tree

ORDER　All dinosaurs are divided into two large groups, based on the shape and position of their hip bones. Saurischians had forward-pointing hip bones, like lizards.

SUBORDER　Sauropodomorphs were long-necked plant-eating dinosaurs.

INFRAORDER　Prosauropods were early relatives and possible ancestors of the giant long-necked sauropods.

FAMILY　A family includes one or more types of closely related dinosaurs.

GENUS　Every dinosaur has a two-word name. The first word tells us what genus, or type, of dinosaur it is. The genus plus the second word are its species—the group of very similar animals it belongs to. (For example, *Plateosaurus engelhardti* is one species of *Plateosaurus*.)

Scientists organize all living things into groups, according to features shared.
This chart shows one way of grouping the early long-necked plant-eaters described in this book.

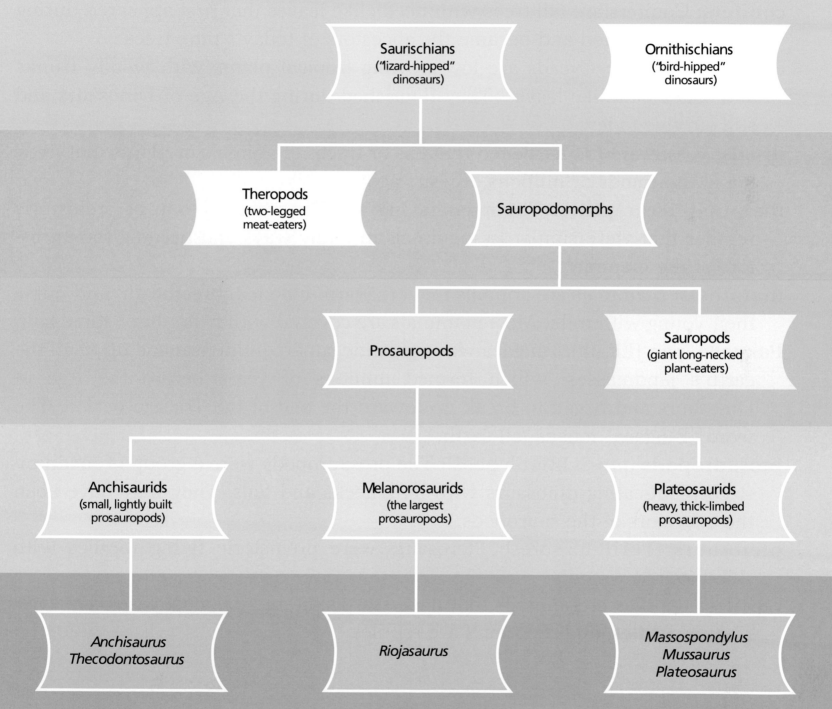

Saurischians
("lizard-hipped"
dinosaurs)

Ornithischians
("bird-hipped"
dinosaurs)

Theropods
(two-legged
meat-eaters)

Sauropodomorphs

Prosauropods

Sauropods
(giant long-necked
plant-eaters)

Anchisaurids
(small, lightly built
prosauropods)

Melanorosaurids
(the largest
prosauropods)

Plateosaurids
(heavy, thick-limbed
prosauropods)

Anchisaurus
Thecodontosaurus

Riojasaurus

Massospondylus
Mussaurus
Plateosaurus

Glossary

conifers: Conifers are tall trees with needlelike leaves that first appeared during the Triassic period and became the ancestors of today's pine trees.

cycads (SIE-kuds)**:** Cycads are low-growing tropical plants with woody trunks and sharp palmlike leaves. They flourished during the Age of Dinosaurs and still survive today.

fossils: Fossils are the hardened remains or traces of animals or plants that lived many thousands or millions of years ago.

mammal-like reptiles: The mammal-like reptiles were a group of prehistoric reptiles that were similar to mammals in many ways and became the ancestors of the mammals.

mammals: Mammals are animals that are warm-blooded, breathe air, and nurse their young with milk. Most mammals are covered with fur or have some hair.

Pangaea (pan-JEE-uh)**:** Pangaea was a gigantic supercontinent made up of all the earth's landmasses, which formed millions of years before the Age of Dinosaurs and began to break up toward the end of the Triassic period. The word "Pangaea" means "all earth."

prosauropods (pro-SORE-uh-pods)**:** The prosauropods were a group of medium-sized plant-eating dinosaurs with long necks and tails. They may have been the ancestors of the sauropods.

pterosaurs (TEHR-uh-sores)**:** Pterosaurs were prehistoric flying reptiles with skin-covered wings.

reptiles: Reptiles are animals that have scaly skin and, in most cases, lay eggs. Lizards, turtles, and dinosaurs are reptiles.

sauropods (SORE-uh-pods): The sauropods were a group of giant long-necked plant-eating dinosaurs that were the longest, tallest, and heaviest animals ever to walk the earth.

stomach stones: Prosauropods and some other plant-eating dinosaurs swallowed stones to help grind up the food in their stomachs. Stomach stones are also called gastroliths.

Triassic (try-ASS-ik) **period:** The Triassic period lasted from about 250 million to 205 million years ago.

Find Out More

BOOKS

Cole, Stephen. *Walking with Dinosaurs: Photo Journal.* New York: Dorling Kindersley, 2000.

Holmes, Thom, and Laurie Holmes. *Gigantic Long-Necked Plant-Eating Dinosaurs.* Berkeley Heights, NJ: Enslow Publishers, 2001.

Lessem, Don. *Scholastic Dinosaurs A to Z.* New York: Scholastic Books, 2003.

Marshall, Chris, ed. *Dinosaurs of the World.* 11 volumes. New York: Marshall Cavendish, 1999.

Matthews, Rupert. *The Jurassic Dinosaurs.* Woodbridge, CT: Blackbirch Press, 2002.

Parker, Steve. *The Early Dinosaurs.* Volume 2, *The Age of the Dinosaurs.* Danbury, CT: Grolier Educational, 2000.

Online Sources*

Dino Directory at http://internt.nhm.ac.uk/jdsml/dino
The Natural History Museum in London, England, created this guide to more than one hundred of the best-known dinosaurs. There are facts, drawings, and photos from museum exhibits featuring several prosauropods, including *Plateosaurus* and *Anchisaurus.*

"Dino" Don's Dinosaur World at http://www.dinosaurdon.com/dinodon
Created by dinosaur expert Don Lessem, this site offers fun facts about dinosaurs, a coloring book, and a dinosaur dictionary.

The Dinosaur Museum at http://www.dinosaur-museum.org
The Dinosaur Museum in Blanding, Utah, explores the history of the prehistoric world through fossils, graphics, and sculptures. Click on "Global Dinosaurs" to see the museum's exhibit of a *Plateosaurus* skeleton.

Project Prosauropod at http://museum.gov.ns.ca/fgm/lab/prosauropod10.html
This Web site from the Fundy Geological Museum of Parrsboro, Nova Scotia, follows the progress of researchers who are investigating a 200-million-year-old prosauropod skeleton. The site is updated every week with new discoveries, photographs, and animations.

Science and Nature: Prehistoric Life at http://www.bbc.co.uk/dinosaurs
This companion site to the BBC television series *Walking with Dinosaurs* presents in-depth information on more than sixty dinosaurs through sound, video, photographs, and interactive games. Click on "Fact Files" for a page on *Plateosaurus* that includes a moving image and video clip.

*Web site addresses sometimes change. The addresses here were all available when this book was sent to press. For more online sources, check with the media specialist at your local library.

Index

About the Author

Virginia Schomp grew up in a quiet suburban town in northeastern New Jersey where eight-ton duck-billed dinosaurs once roamed. In first grade, she discovered that she loved reading and writing, and in sixth grade she was voted "class bookworm," because she always had her nose in a book. Today she is a freelance writer who has published more than fifty books for young readers on topics including animals, careers, American history, and ancient cultures. Ms. Schomp lives in the Catskill Mountain region of New York State with her husband, Richard, and their son, Chip.

Dinosaurs lived millions of years ago. Everything we know about them—how they looked, walked, ate, fought, mated, and raised their young—comes from educated guesses by the scientists who discover and study fossils. The information in this book is based on what most scientists believe right now. Tomorrow or next week or next year, new discoveries could lead to new ideas. So keep your eyes and ears open for news flashes from the prehistoric world!

Marshall Cavendish Benchmark
99 White Plains Road
Tarrytown, New York 10591-9001
www.marshallcavendish.us

Text copyright © 2006 by Marshall Cavendish Corporation
Map copyright © 2006 by Marshall Cavendish Corporation
Map and Dinosaur Family Tree by Robert Romagnoli

Library of Congress Cataloging-in-Publication Data
Schomp, Virginia.
Plateosaurus : and other early long-necked plant-eaters / by Virginia Schomp.
p. cm. — (Prehistoric world)
Includes bibliographical references and index.
Summary: "Describes the physical characteristics and behavior of Plateosaurus and other early long-necked plant-eaters"—Provided by publisher.
ISBN-13 978-0-7614-2008-8
ISBN 0–7614–2008–8
1. Plateosaurus—Juvenile literature. 2. Dinosaurs—Juvenile literature. I. Title. II. Series.
QE862.S3S3863 2005
567.913—dc22
2004027726

Front cover and pages 2-3: *Plateosaurus*   Back cover: Anchisaurus

Front cover illustration from Natural History Museum Photo Library, London
Back cover illustration courtesy of Marshall Cavendish Corporation
The illustrations and photographs in this book are used by permission and through the courtesy of the following: © John Sibbick 1985. Reproduced by permission of Salamander, an imprint of Chrysalis Books Group Plc.: 2-3, 12-13; Marshall Cavendish Corporation: 4-5, 8-9, 10, 16-17, 18, 22-23, 24-25; © Douglas Henderson from *Dinosaurs, A Global View*: 7; Ludek Pesek / Photo Researchers, Inc.: 15; Laurie O'Keefe/ Photo Researchers, Inc.: 19; Jan Sovak: 21

Printed in China

3 5 6 4 2